Seek God

JILL LOWRY

ISBN-13: 978-1-7371825-3-5

Seek God

Copyright © 2023 by Jill Lowry.
All rights reserved. Except for use in any review, the reproduction or utilization of this work in whole or in part in any form by any electronic, mechanical or other means, now known or hereinafter invented, including xerography, photocopying, and recording, or in any information storage or retrieval system, is forbidden without the written permission of
Jill Lowry.

Cover & Scripture Images Designed by Kerry Prater.
Interior Design by Katharine E. Hamilton

Scripture quotations are from the ESV® Bible (The Holy Bible, English Standard Version®), copyright © 2001 by Crossway, a publishing ministry of Good News Publishers. Used by permission. All rights reserved.

DEDICATION

This book is dedicated to my Lord who has revived my heart and given me faith that can move mountains.

Introduction

How do you hear God's voice? Have you ever wondered if He will speak to you? God does speak…but are you listening? To hear God, you must seek Him and call upon Him. But how do you do that? PRAY, PRAY, PRAY!

Yes, simply stated, the way to hear God speak begins with prayer. Are you praying? Prayer is the way to communicate with God. He wants you to seek Him by calling upon Him. Prayer brings intimacy with the One who knows you best. He wants to hear from you so He can share great and wonderful things with you. He will speak, so listen expectantly as you pray.

"Call to me and I will answer you, and will tell you great and hidden things that you have not known."
Jeremiah 33:3

God also speaks through His Word. Open your Bible and read the love letters He has written for you. Know that He loves you. Hear His voice in His beautiful treasures of truth written just for you. His promises will give you hope and will bring you answers to life's questions.

"Your word is a lamp to my feet and a light to my path."
Psalm 119:105

Throughout the Bible, we read about God speaking to people. God spoke to Moses in a flame of fire in the burning bush. His powerful presence was there as Moses heard God's voice loud and clear. Moses was seeking God and he heard God call his name. He came close to His voice, but hid his face from God because he was afraid. Like Moses, we let fear set in, think we are not worthy, and we hide from the Voice of Truth. But God, who is always faithful, will never leave us. God told Moses that He wanted him to bring His people out of Egypt. Moses heard the request but still was unsure what to say to the people who needed to be rescued. When Moses asked God what to say to His people,

God said to Moses, "I AM WHO I AM." And He said, 'Say to the people of Israel, I AM has sent me to you.'"
Exodus 3:14

I AM is the one who speaks to you as well. When you know Him, I AM will be with you. Seek God. He is right there with you.
"But I will be with you…"
Exodus 3:12

How to Use this Devotional

Before beginning this devotional, pray that God will speak clearly to you. Ask Him to show you what He wants you to see and hear as you read and ponder the questions at the end of each one. Then, meditate on the Scripture on each page. As you read with a grateful and prayerful heart, the Holy Spirit will enlighten you to see with spiritual eyes. He will speak as you keep Him close. Focus on what you hear that jumps off the page and into your heart.

As you read the part beginning with "I AM…", read it as if God is speaking to you. I have opened my prayer journal of what God has spoken to me as I prayed and listened in my spirit. I wanted to share these words with you to build up your faith and your love for God who loves to spend time with you. Remember, He is available to you 24/7. Seek God with all your heart so He will revive you!

"You will seek me and find me, when you seek me with all your heart." Jeremiah 29:13

Why I Wrote this Devotional

I wrote this devotional to help you in your journey to hear more of God's voice. There have been times in my life that I was not hearing His voice. But, now I realize that I was not seeking God or calling upon

Him in those times. I was also seeking other voices and placing more weight on pleasing others, only listening to their advice and wisdom and not God's voice. Because I desperately wanted to hear God speak truth to me, I began praying more and spending quality time with God each day in His Word. I made God my priority! He became the first one I spoke to each morning and the last one I reached out to each night. I talked with God all day. He became my best friend. As I changed my priorities, God changed me and His voice became louder and stronger in my spirit and I was filled with the Holy Spirit's guidance.

Spend time with God each day in this devotional, in your Bible, in prayer, and I AM WHO I AM will speak to you. Keep close to I AM and seek more of Him each day. Listen and hear how much He loves you!

> ***"Speak, for your servant hears."***
> ***1 Samuel 3:10***

Much love to you my friends,
Jill Lowry

I
AM
WHO
I
AM

When you seek after someone, you search until you find them.

**"Seek the LORD while he may be found; call upon him while he is near."
Isaiah 55:6**

I AM...near to you and want to bring you closer to My love. I will hold you close even when you struggle. I will celebrate with you as you invite Me into your life. I will give you the choice to live closer to Me, though I yearn for you to be so. As you lean in, you will see Me. As you come closer, you will hear Me. My voice comforts and consoles. There is no place you can go that I am not near to you.

Are you seeking Me with all your heart?

I want you to seek Me and live abundantly with the guarantee of hope and the promise of eternal life. My heart is close to yours.

What can you do to seek more of God?

Journal ways you want to be more devoted to God beginning today.

As you seek Me, you will taste the sweetest gift of love.

**"Oh, taste and see that the LORD is good! Blessed is the man who takes refuge in him!"
Psalm 34:8**

I AM...waiting for you to receive what I want to give you. My love is sweeter than anything you will ever taste. It is yours as you seek Me. Let go of the bitterness you have toward those people that is pulling you away from Me. Hold on to hope that is yours in Me. Say hello to your new life that is grounded and rooted in My love. Give Me the time and attention you are giving to other things.

Can you see Me?

Taste and see the glory that is granted to you as a child of Mine. You are My beloved.

How can you taste the sweetness of God's love for you?
Pray that you will take time to rest in His love throughout today.

When you find the love you are seeking, you hold it close.

**"You shall love the LORD your God with all your heart and with all your soul and with all your might."
Deuteronomy 6:5**

I AM …right beside you. Do you know My love? I know you have been restless and need to feel My presence. I am the light shining in your heart. Seek Me and rest in My love. Behold My love, and let it settle within you. Do not worry about tomorrow.

Do you know how much I love you?

Love Me and see how close I am to you. Touch My love, and let it bloom in Your heart and warm your soul. I love you, dear one.

Are you more worried about tomorrow or enjoying the presence of God's love?

Write down at least three worries you will give to God today.

Trust requires a surrender of self to seek more of God.

"**Trust in the LORD with all your heart, and do not lean on your own understanding. In all your ways acknowledge him, and he will make straight your paths.**"
Proverbs 3:5-6

I AM …able to do more as you trust Me. If you will not let Me in, I cannot show you the great and mighty things I want to accomplish in and through you. Do not be afraid. A little bit of trust goes a long way. Give it *all* to Me. I will take your burdens and show you the path.

What is weighing so heavy on your mind?

Trust Me, dear one. It is time to let it all go. You are too blessed to be stressed, dear child.

Is your stress keeping you awake at night? Begin asking God to carry these burdens as you promise to surrender all to Him today.

God removes guilt from the souls of those who seek grace.

"But God, being rich in mercy, because of the great love with which he loved us, even when we were dead in our trespasses, made us alive together with Christ-by grace you have been saved."
Ephesians 2:4-5

I AM ...rich in mercy and full of grace. Remember My sacrifice for you on the cross. I paid it all so you can be free from sin. By My stripes, you have been healed.

Are you seeking grace from Me?

Let Me hold you and take your sins. There is nothing you can do to make Me love you more, and there is nothing you have done to make Me love you less. I have saved you by grace, precious one. You are alive in Christ, lavished in My redeeming love.

What past sin is holding you captive?

Pray that you will receive God's grace and forgive yourself today just as God has forgiven you.

I AM THE BREAD OF LIFE

Delight in knowing God, and His desires will become yours.

**"Delight yourself in the LORD, and he will give you the desires of your heart."
Psalm 37:4**

I AM ...close to you as you delight in Me. I hear your heart as you seek Me with tenderness and devotion. I will whisper gently as we walk hand in hand through mountains and valleys. I will never leave or forsake you.

Do you want Me close to you?

Come to Me and let Me share My heart with yours. I have much to tell you and show you. Many do not find Me because they are not listening with their hearts. Make the choice to seek Me and you will know My desires for you, dear child. My desires will become yours as you stay yoked to Me.

What are the desires of your heart?

Pray for God to show you if these desires are His desires for you.

God speaks when your soul is still before Him.

**"Be still, and know that I am God."
Psalm 46:10**

I AM …here for you. I know right where the pain is the deepest and the problem is the hardest. I see your tears and know what you are going through. These challenges will be part of your story.

What is your biggest challenge right now?

Remember how you found ME faithful before and know that I will be faithful again. I want you to stay faithful, too, and keep close to Me. I will fight for you. Be still and know that I am the God who loves you even when you do not think you deserve it. Rest in my grace knowing that I am with you always, blessed one. Have faith in Me. I am writing your story.

Are you taking time to be still before God?

Make note of the times you are still today "with God."

When you seek God first, He makes a way.

**"But seek first the kingdom of God and his righteousness, and all these things will be added to you."
Matthew 6:33**

I AM…speaking to you. As you seek Me first, I will show you the way. I have a plan for you that includes Me, but you are looking to the right and to the left for all the answers instead of fixing your eyes on Me. All the things you are seeking are right in front of you.

Do you hear My voice?

I am singing a symphony of love songs to you. Listen, My child. My love is calling you closer. My melody will put you on the path where I am. I will meet you on the narrow road where the path of life begins and ends with Me.

Are you listening for God's voice?

Pray that God will speak to you today as you promise to listen.

Every step closer to God grows your faith.

"And without faith it is impossible to please him, for whoever would draw near to God must believe that he exists and that he rewards those who seek him."
Hebrews 11:6

I AM …giving you the faith you need to keep going. My reward to you for seeking Me is the deep faith growing inside of you. Keep drawing closer to Me. I need you to stay faithful even when others do not have faith. I will finish the work I am doing in you. Trust Me in the process and believe Me.

Do you have faith in Me?

I am working all things out in ways you may not see now, but someday you will. Move closer and wait for Me with eyes of faith. I am speaking love to you faithful one. I will do the impossible.

Are you ready to grow your faith and relationship with God?

List some active steps of faith you will take today.

God gives strength to those who seek Him.

"Seek the LORD and his strength; seek his presence continually!"
1 Chronicles 16:11

I AM…infusing you with strength because you are seeking Me. I want you to feel the winds of My Spirit and the rains of My love. I have so much to pour into you. Believe I am not finished molding you. If you open your heart, seek more of Me, and live with the power of the Holy Spirit in you, I will direct your steps and guide you into all truth.

Are you seeking My truth?

Build your life on My truth and unfailing love. I will fill you with all that you need. Seek My presence in all that you do to gain new strength and peace for all your days.

What is zapping your strength?

Ask God to take this away and believe that He will infuse you with more strength today.

I AM THE LIGHT OF THE WORLD

Those who seek will find God waiting for them through the open door to life.

"Ask, and it will be given to you; seek, and you will find; knock, and it will be opened to you."
Matthew 7:7

I AM...waiting for you to ask Me for what is on your heart. It is time to cling to Me instead of empty promises. Rely on Me and believe what I speak over you.

Why have you been so afraid to knock on My door?

I am ready to fulfill all your needs. I know what you need even before you ask. My Word never fails. Ask and I will answer you. Seek and you will find Me through the open door before you. I love you and am there for you. Ask Me for what you need and wait for My answers.

What have you been afraid to ask of God?

Write down the details of your boldest prayers and pray them today.

The nearer God is to you, the dearer He becomes.

"Draw near to God, and he will draw near to you. Cleanse your hands, you sinners, and purify your hearts, you double-minded."
James 4:8

I AM...so close to you. I have rushed to meet you in the places where you live. Your choice to repent and invite Me into your life has been the best decision you will ever make.

What do you need to tell Me?

Do not be afraid to speak to Me. I am nearer to you, so let go and let Me love you. Come closer to Me and I will bring calmness to your soul. My peace I will give to you. Let not your heart be troubled anymore. Love has come to rescue you.

What does drawing nearer to God look like for you?

Ask God to show you ways you can come closer to His love today.

The presence of God will be with you when you press into His peace.

"You keep him in perfect peace whose mind is stayed on you, because he trusts in you."
Isaiah 26:3

I AM...here to give you peace as you keep your mind centered on Me. I hear your prayers and have listened to your cries for mercy. If you trust Me, I will be the presence of peace no matter what you are facing.

What problem are you facing?

Let my peace rule in your heart and your mind. Do not listen to the other voices that interfere with the peace I have for you. My peace is perfect and present. Seek Me, precious one. I will give you My peace.

Whose voices are you listening to?

List all these voices. Pray that today you will listen to the voice of truth, the Lord God who brings peace.

Waiting on the God of hope brings your heart closer to His.

"For God alone, O my soul, wait in silence, for my hope is from him."
Psalm 62:5

I AM...carrying hope for you. Take My light of hope and let its flame spark a fire in your soul. Only I can lift you up to greater heights. With Me, you will rise above the fray and fear to a place where hope reigns.

Do you need more hope?

Look to Me and find the hope you need. You do not have to be weary and tired from all the busyness of life. I will help you, when you trust Me. I speak hope to the hopeless. Wait on Me.

Are you hopeful for what God has promised you?

List some promises of God you are clinging to today.

There is no place for fear when faith rises.

"For not all have faith. But the Lord is faithful. He will establish you and guard you against the evil one."
2 Thessalonians 3:2-3

I AM...helping you to see the truth as I test your faith. My faithful hand is upon you even in situations where you face fear. Trouble cannot stop those who walk by faith.

Are you more fearful or faithful?

Let your faith rise over fear and listen to My truth. I will show you what faith can do for you. Have faith, precious one. I am doing something new in you and it is more marvelous and powerful than anything you can ever imagine. Not all have faith, but I am faithful. Faith over fear!

What or who are you afraid of?

List your fears and pray that God will help you release them today.

I AM THE GATE OF THE SHEEPFOLD

Pray like you believe and live like you believe God will answer.

**"But the hour is coming and is now here, when true worshippers will worship the Father in spirit and truth, for the Father is seeking such people to worship him."
John 4:23**

I AM...listening to you, dear one. Keep lifting up your prayers. Believe I will answer and thank Me before you know how I will respond. I am watching and waiting to hear, not only your prayers, but your praises.

Are you worshipping Me?

I hear each time you lift up a prayer to Me. Watch Me as I work all things out. Give Me time to make miracles out of mountains. I will let you know when it is time to go. Until then, keep praying with all of your heart for what is on your heart and watch me move.

What mountain have you been praying for God to move?

Pray throughout today about what is on your heart and believe that God can miraculously move it!

Turn your worry list into a prayer list.

"Do not be anxious about anything, but in everything by prayer and supplication with thanksgiving let your requests be made known God."
Philippians 4:6

I AM...here to take your anxieties and burdens. Give them to Me. You have too many worries weighing you down. If you let go, I will help you. Take Me with you *wherever* you go. There is no place that I will not be right there with you.

Do you hear Me calling you?

Listen with your heart and let Me fight your battles. You only have to remain silent and steadfast. I know how to help you, if you will ask Me. Praise Me, for the victory is already won for you. I am above all and in all. Come closer and find all you need in Me.

Have you been anxious?

Write down your worries and make it your prayer list today.

There is a moment of release before the rescue.

**"He brought me out into a broad place; he rescued me, because He delighted in me."
Psalm 18:19**

I AM...hovering over you with delight, my precious child. You have let Me rescue you because you listened and let go. I will never let go of you.

Do you see that this struggle has brought you closer to Me?

Even when you did not understand, I knew what you needed. I will rescue you because you have listened and released control over to Me, your Redeemer. I am your rock and refuge. Believe all things are possible with Me!

What do you need rescuing from?

Write a prayer of rescue and ask God to release you from it today.

With Christ, you will go out with tears, but return with joy!

**"Rejoice with those who rejoice, weep with those who weep."
Romans 12:15**

I AM…bringing joy out of your tears. Let Me love you so I can show you what I see. Your heart will break for what breaks mine as you see with new spiritual eyes.

Do you see those who are weeping and those who are rejoicing?

I see them, too. Weep with them. Comfort them with your prayers of love. Rejoice with them and lift up your shouts of praise to Me! Worship Me together, as one body of Christ in the bond of peace. Let My joy flood your souls and your tears of sadness will turn into shouts of joy!

Are there people you know who are sad now? What about those who have had answered prayers and are praising God?

Write down their names and pray for them. Now, praise God for His answers!

God's waiting room is your opportunity to grow closer to Him.

**"I wait for the LORD, my soul waits, and in his word I hope."
Psalm 130:5**

I AM…right here with you, My child, even as you wait. You will hear My voice in the stillness of your soul and in the place where you wait. My waiting room is not a place for you to grow impatient, but a place where you can find more of Me.

How long have you been waiting?

Stay here a little longer and see what happens. You will find a place of peace that cannot be explained. You will find hope when others say there is no hope. You will experience restoration of your soul as You wait and watch for Me. You will certainly find Me as you seek Me with all of your heart!

What are you waiting for right now?

Write down how long you have been waiting and ask God to give you more patience and faith today as you wait with hope.

Peace is possible when you walk through the open door where Jesus is waiting for you.

"Peace I leave with you; my peace I give to you. Not as the world gives do I give to you. Let not your hearts be troubled, neither let them be afraid."
John 14:27

I AM...waiting for you to come to Me. My peace awaits, if you will say yes and walk through the open door. Do not be afraid to come to Me. I have the peace you have been searching everywhere to find. I am your peace. Keep searching for Me and you will find Me.

How long will you stay unsettled?

Settle your heart by letting Me show you the way to peace as your Prince of Peace. There is no room for fear because I am near.

Where do you need peace in your life right now?

Be still and pray and let the peace of Christ wash over you today.

I AM THE GOOD SHEPHERD

There is new life for you right now when you live with Christ in you.

**"I came that they may have life and have it abundantly."
John 10:10**

I AM…eager to give you new life as a child of Mine. Let Me revive you. Let Me refresh you with new hope. There is abundant life and unspeakable joy where I am.

Do you see how I am making all things new, including you?

Say yes to newness and let go and let Me show you the way to abundant life. I am the way, the truth, and the life. I am the only way to experience life to the fullest. Abundant life is yours in Me. Be refreshed in My love for you, and I will lead you to green pastures and still waters that will restore your soul.

Describe abundant life.

Ask God to fill you with new life in Him today.

When you give God all your cares, He will carefully lift you up.

**"Casting all your anxieties on him, because he cares for you."
1 Peter 5:7**

I AM…to your left and to your right. I am in front of you and behind you. I am beside you and over you. I am in you, my dear child. I am everywhere with you. Let Me take over and help you. I will be your Helper in trouble and your Comforter in times of need.

What anxieties do you have right now?

Cast them on Me so I can strengthen you with My power. I am present with you when you let go and let Me work all things out. Do not try to do these things alone. Give Me the burdens that are weighing so heavily on you. Let Me take the wheel. Stand by Me and with Me. I will never let you go.

What burdens are weighing on you today?

List each one and draw a cross in the center as you cast each one to God.

When Christ is in you, His light is the brightest light around you.

"In the same way, let your light shine before others, so that they may see your good works and give glory to your Father who is in heaven."
Matthew 5:16

I AM...shining in you so that you can shine My light in the darkness. It is time to come out of the dark and into the light. Others can see Me when they see the rays of light reflecting from the good works you are doing.

What good works are you doing?

Keep doing good and spreading hope. I see what you are doing every moment. I know how you want to help others step out of the dark and into My light. They will come to Me if you keep spreading the light of My love. Press on and let others see Me in you!

Where can you spread the light of Christ?

Ask God to show you who needs to see His light today and go shine for His glory!

Joy is found where Jesus is.

**"You make known to me the path of life; in your presence there is fullness of joy; at your right hand are pleasures forevermore."
Psalm 16:11**

I AM…your joy! Let Me in your life so I can show you what joy I have to give to you. I want you to sit in My presence so I can show you the joyful path of life. I am right here for you. Listen, dear child, and let Me give you My joy that is never ending.

Is your joy with Me?

There are things holding you back from Me. I can fill the empty places in your heart with more of Me. Run away from the other things pulling you down, and run to Me. I will give you all that you need!

Are you a joy maker or a joy stealer?

Ask Jesus to give you opportunities to bring joy to someone today.

Your impossibilities are possible with God.

**"For nothing will be impossible with God."
Luke 1:37**

I AM…speaking to you. Listen to Me and hear Me speak life to you. That problem you are trying to fix cannot be done without Me. If you will seek Me, I will help you. I have been waiting for you to ask Me for what is on your heart. Let go and let Me take that burden from you. I can do what is impossible for man. I have done so much for you and have much more to do in you.

What is it that you need?

Ask Me, dear child, so that I can give you what you need. I am your Way Maker and Miracle Worker. Nothing is impossible with Me!

What do you need that seems impossible?

Write down that impossibility and believe it can be possible with God.

When you stand firm with God, He will set you free.

"For freedom Christ has set us free; stand firm therefore, and do not submit again to a yoke of slavery."
Galatians 5:1

I AM...the key to freedom. You have been searching far and wide for things only I can give you. Stand firm, therefore, and do not let others talk you out of standing *with* Me. I am for you. I want what is best for you. I will give you freedom when you make the choice to stand *with* Me.

Are you standing with Me?

I gave you My Son, Jesus, so that you could be free from the slavery of sin and shame. He has taken all for you. Remember this truth and be yoked to your Savior, Jesus Christ, who will set you free once and for all!

What do you want to be free from today?

List these things and pray for God to set you free!

I
AM
THE RESURRECTION AND THE LIFE

Believe God can do more for you with His power at work in you.

"Now to him who is able to do far more abundantly than all we ask or think, according to the power at work within us." Ephesians 3:20

I AM...able to do *more* in you. Let me work in you. I know what you think I can do, but I can do even *more* with My power at work in you!

Why are you settling for less by trying to do everything by yourself?

I see you trying to control it all without Me. All you need to do is let Me in all areas of your life and give Me room to work. I can do even more than you can believe if you will just trust Me and activate My power, the Holy Spirit, already inside you. Give it all to Me and see what I can do for you!

Have you activated the power of the Holy Spirit in you?

Pray a prayer of surrender and ask for His power to be active and working in you today.

When your faith rises, fear disappears, and your future is bright.

**"Take heart; it is I. Do not be afraid."
Mark 6:50**

I AM…right beside you, dear child. Rest in My presence and put your full faith and trust in Me. I will never leave or forsake you when you invite Me in your heart. The world has been telling you that it is not possible to live by faith, but I say, let go of fear and fix your eyes on Me.

Are your eyes on Me or the problem?

I know what you are facing. I see your struggle. I know your pain. But I also see your future which is full of hope and peace. Take heart, and believe, and watch your fear disappear right before your eyes.

Are you in pain right now and need healing? What healing are you praying to receive?

Pray that God will take away your pain and instill new faith in you today.

When you trust God and walk by faith, you will certainly find Him.

**"For we walk by faith, not by sight."
2 Corinthians 5:7**

I AM...opening the door for you. Try walking through My door even without knowing all the details. I know the greater plan for your good and My glory.

Will you go, even when you cannot see all that is in front of you?

Remember, I am always there for you. I am in front of you and behind you. My hand is on your shoulder beside you. Go with faith on the journey marked just for you. It has blessings in store that you will not want to miss. If you go, I will show you great and mighty things you have yearned to know. Trust Me, walk by faith, and stay on the narrow path that leads to Me.

Have you trusted God to help you even when you cannot see all the details?

Pray for guidance about where you need more trust today.

Work heartily for God who works mightily in you.

**"Whatever you do, work heartily, as for the Lord and not for men."
Colossians 3:23**

I AM…working in you. Do you hear Me? I am waiting for you to listen so I can tell you great and mighty things I want to do in and through you. I know what you are facing and how hard it is. Let Me show you the way.

Are you looking for Me?

There is hope over the challenges you face. There is life where I am. Come to Me. I promise to help you see the right way to take if you will set your eyes on Me. I am right here beside you. Do you see Me?

Where do you see God at work around you?

List those opportunities and go join Him in the work He is already doing today.

Strength comes as you seek the presence of God and forge forward with faith.

"But you, take courage! Do not let your hands be weak, for your work shall be rewarded."
2 Chronicles 15:7

I AM...right here with you. I know that you feel tired and weary from all that you are doing. I see how people have let you down and have not been there for you. But I promise to be there for you! We can do this together!

Will you trust Me?

With Me, all things are possible and will work out in My will for you. I see everything you are doing. I know what you have faced and will face in the present and future even before you see it. Trust Me, seek more of My strength, and forge forward with faith.

Do you need more energy to finish the work you are doing right now?

Ask God to give you more strength to keep going. Pray that you will not give up.

If you want forgiveness, forgive them, and believe God will forgive you.

"Be kind to one another, tenderhearted, forgiving one another, as God in Christ forgave you."
Ephesians 4:32

I AM…waiting for you to forgive them. I know you are hurt and do not see why they did these things to you. Do not try to understand; just simply forgive them. I will deal with their hardness of heart. I will help you with these difficult challenges.

Will you forgive?

If you let go of your anger and offense, I will set you free. I will also soften your heart toward them so that what they did will not bother you anymore. Give Me the burdens, forgive them in your heart, and I will forgive you.

Who do you need to forgive?

Write down their names and pray for them.

Persistent prayer brings more hope and joy even in the hardest times.

"Rejoice in hope, be patient in tribulation, be constant in prayer."
Romans 12:12

I AM…the one who listens to you. Keep praying, knowing that I hear you. I am sorry you are going through the pain of losing someone close to you. I know how hard it is to say goodbye. But remember, there is *always* hope if you turn to Me. I will bring you joy even in the toughest times.

Are you lifting up your prayers to Me?

If you stay patient and persistent in prayer, your tears will turn to joy. I will come when you call. I see your tears and your fears. I will wipe them all away and bring you new joy. So, rejoice in the hope that is found in Me. Look up, My dear child.

Where do you need more hope?

Believe God will give you more hope today as you trust Him and pray.

When you give from your heart, you will grow closer to God.

**"For God loves a cheerful giver."
2 Corinthians 9:7**

I AM…watching and waiting for you to give without expecting anything in return. I love cheerful givers, who know that it is more blessed to give than to receive. Each time you give, you give to Me. When you serve others, you are serving Me.

Who do you see that needs you?

When you love like Me, you see like Me. I have come to live in your heart so that you will have full joy and abundant life. Give and serve and you will experience this joy flooding your soul. Find more blessings by opening your heart to more of Me!

Who and where can you serve?

Ask God to show you where He needs you and begin a new season of cheerful giving today.

I
AM
THE
WAY,
TRUTH
AND LIFE

Believe that if God brings you to it, He will bring you through it.

**"Behold, I am the LORD, the God of all flesh. Is anything too hard for me?"
Jeremiah 32:27**

I AM…already working it out for you. I have brought you through so much already and will help you get through this too. Do not worry, but trust Me, dear one. Nothing is too hard for Me. Those hurdles will help you rise above the challenges.

Do you believe that I will be with you even when you are tired and tempted to quit?

I promise to keep a close eye on you as you run your race. Keep going, one leap at a time with My lead: sure and steady. You will not fall when you keep in step with Me.

What challenge are you facing today?

Write it here, give it to God, and put your focus on God instead of the storm.

The constant love of God is so powerful and perfect.

**"For I am sure that neither death nor life, nor angels nor rulers, nor things present nor things to come, nor powers, nor height nor depth, nor anything else in all creation, will be able to separate us from the love of God in Christ Jesus our Lord."
Romans 8:38-39**

I AM…rushing in to save you. I will chase you until you find Me. I will not stop pursuing you. Nothing can separate you from My love, not anyone or anything.

Who is trying to push you away from Me?

Come closer to Me and believe I will overpower you with My unstoppable love. My love for you keeps growing, never doubt it. My love will be with you, and in you, wherever you go. I love you, dear child.

Do you love God with all your heart?

Write a love letter to God telling Him how much you love Him right now.

Life is abundant when Christ is at the center.

"For me to live is Christ, and to die is gain."
Philippians 1:21

I AM...cheering for you. I am your best yes. In other words, You can count on Me to encourage you. I have your best interest at heart and will not let the enemy torment you. Remain close to Me. I have life to give you.

What are you worried about?

Do not fret, but set your sights on Me. There is no other way to new life than through Me. Choose to live abundantly with Me. I can give you all you need, indeed. Watch Me strengthen you with new joy as you seek Me with all your heart.

Who is stealing your joy today?

Pray for God to help you set your sights on Him and not those who are trying to distract you.

When your thoughts are on praiseworthy things, your mouth speaks praises to God.

"Finally, brothers, whatever is true, whatever is honorable, whatever is just, whatever is pure, whatever is lovely, whatever is commendable, if there is any excellence, if there is anything worthy of praise, think about these things."
Philippians 4:8

I AM...the giver of all good gifts. Let me give you yours. My gifts come wrapped in grace and tied with a bow of love.

Will you receive the gifts I have for you?

When you open My gifts, your mind will be focused on the things that are praiseworthy and true, and your mouth will sing praises to Me. I am just, pure, lovely, and commendable. Focus on Me, and you will find gratitude in every moment.

Are you more focused on what is worthy of praise or what you are worried about today?

Make of list of your God-given gifts and thank God for each of them.

Travel on the narrow road where God's gate is open wide for you.

"For the gate is narrow and the way is hard that leads to life, and those who find it are few."
Matthew 7:14

I AM...opening the gate and waiting for you on the road less traveled. I am here with you every step of the way. Enter the narrow gate and wait for Me. Do not fear, because I am near and will be there to guide you to all truth. Those who find life know Me and trust Me.

Why are you hesitating?

Your journey has already been planned before You were born. Step out and find security with Me. I am where the joy of the journey begins and ends.

How will you bring Jesus on the journey with you?

List ways that you can seek more of Him right now.

I AM THE DOOR

Those who put their hope in God will find joy and peace in life's journey.

"May the God of hope fill you with all joy and peace in believing, so that by the power of the Holy Spirit you may abound in hope."
Romans 15:13

I AM...giving you My gift of hope. Take it and let it fill all the places of your soul. You have been searching for things that only I can give you. Do not let others stop you from trusting only Me. Be obedient and let faith carry you.

Do you hear Me calling you to more hope?

I am the God of the impossible. I can do all things in you only if you let Me in. Surrender all to Me. I will take all your burdens from you. Draw to My hope and be filled with joy and peace from the power of the Holy Spirit.

Are you listening to God telling you there is still hope?

Let the God of hope fill you with His peace and joy so that you may abound in hope.

When your heart is close to God, you will strive to trust and obey His Word.

**"With my whole heart I seek you; let me not wander from your commandments!"
Psalm 119:10**

I AM…close to you. Do you hear Me? I am whispering truth in your ear. I am holding your hand close. I am covering you with my grace and love.

Do you hear My voice?

Stay focused on Me, ears listening, so that I can speak life and peace over you. I will not lead you astray or tell you things that are not true. Keep close to Me so I can speak to you. Listen with your whole heart, so I can show you the way. My path is the right way to go even if it seems hard. Stay on the right path. I will not leave you, dear child.

What truth is God whispering to you right now?

Listen with your heart and write down what comes to your mind.

Being kind makes your day brighter and your heart overflow with joy.

**"So whatever you wish that others would do to you, do also to them."
Matthew 7:12**

I AM…looking at your heart and I see your kindness flow from within. When you give out of the goodness of your heart, you will be blessed, indeed. What you give will come back to you in ways you cannot even imagine.

Who can you give My love to today?

Give and let My love flow within you. Reach for Me and let Me show you the ways I need you to help others see Me. Take time to be kind and see how joy continues to flood your soul. My gift to you is this overflowing joy that remains. I am where the joy is found!

Who can you be kind to today?

Ask God to reveal someone who needs your kindness. Write their name here.

You can see clearly when you let the light of God's Word shine within you.

**"Your word is a lamp to my feet and a light to my path."
Psalm 119:105**

I AM...shining over you so you can see me. I have numerous things to show you in My Word of truth. Keep looking for Me and know I will light up your life. Follow Me.

Do you see Me?

There are multiple paths to take, but only one way that leads to life. Follow the light to find My way. Follow the path where I am. Do not get off the lighted path, but stay close to Me. I will shine life into you, My dear child.

What scripture from the Word of God do you need to cling to right now?

Write it here and try to memorize it.

Put on God's love and you will find the answer you are looking for.

**"So now faith, hope, and love abide, these three; but greatest of these is love."
1 Corinthians 13:13**

I AM…full of great love for you. Soak up My love and rest in Me. The greatest of all gifts is the love I have given you. Now, give My love to others so the fragrance of love will spread. Secure yourself in My love. Wait on Me instead of waiting on the world.

Are you waiting for Me?

You will know the love I have for you when you take time to abide in My never-ending love. Be secure in Me. Give Me your heart so you can receive your greatest gift!

Do you know how much God loves you?

Soak up His love and thank God for His everlasting love for you.

I AM THE TRUE VINE

Turn to your God of all mercy and comfort who will provide the healing you need.

"If my people who are called by my name humble themselves, and pray and seek my face and turn from their wicked ways, then I will hear from heaven and will forgive their sin and heal their land."
2 Chronicles 7:14

I AM...your healer. I will heal your brokenness if you humbly seek My face and pray. I need to hear what is on your heart. Ask, repent, and seek Me.

Have you asked Me to help you?

I want you to turn away from sin and give your heart to Me. I see the temptations you are facing. I will help you and heal all that is broken. I know what you are facing and will face in the future. Let My face shine upon you and give you peace and healing.

Do you need healing?

Pray that God will heal you and believe in His power to heal you today.

When you open your ears and your heart to God, you will hear clearer because God is nearer.

**"He who has ears to hear, let him hear."
Luke 8:8**

I AM…speaking clearly to you, dear child. I am not angry with you but am speaking truth in love. There are times when I must discipline you because you are going the wrong way and listening to other voices around you. My voice is the one you must listen to.

Are you listening to Me?

Take heart and open your ears to My voice. I am calling You closer to the Way that leads to life with me, so do not wander further off the path. I am right here with you. Come with all Your sins, sorrows, and shame, and I will hold you in My loving, grace-filled arms.

Do you need more grace?

Ask God for grace and confess what comes to your mind.

When you trust Jesus, there is no place for fear.

"The Lord is my light and my salvation; whom shall I fear? The LORD is the stronghold of my life; of whom shall I be afraid?
Psalm 27:1

I AM…your stronghold. Give me Your hand and I will strengthen you and take away all your fears. You have hidden yourself from Me instead of letting Me help you. I am your very present help in trouble. Let My light and love shine in and around you.

Will you choose to turn to Me?

There is nothing that can take away My love. Do not turn away, but turn toward Me. I have forgiven You and am giving you grace upon grace. Let Me in and be illuminated with My light.

What fears are you facing right now?

Write them down and let them go. God wants to take them from you.

When you follow Jesus, He forgives you.

"Take heart, daughter; your faith has made you well."
Matthew 9:22

I AM…healing you from the inside out. As you faithfully follow Me, I will do something new in you. I hear your cries for healing and peace. I will open Your heart and give you peace for your soul.

Where do you need healing?

Ask Me and believe that I can heal you. I need you to keep your faith, take heart, and follow Me to freedom and peace where I will heal your soul. Your healing rests in My arms of grace. Will you believe that I can heal you?

Do you need forgiveness and healing?

Ask God to forgive you. He wants to heal you and bring peace to you.

God makes the impossible possible.

**"What is impossible with man is possible with God."
Luke 18:27**

I AM...going to do something new in you. I want you to believe that all things are possible for Me. Let go of your worries and fears so I can show you great and magnificent things that I have in store for you. Behind every fear is a miracle happening for you.

Do you need a miracle?

Give Me your burdens and realize that sometimes you must face these challenges to find the right path you are meant to be on. Be confident in My love and stay faithful to Me for what is to come. I will make all things new for you as You remain close to Me!

Do you need a miracle right now?

Believe that God wants to show you something amazing and keep following Him to see it.

When you let the light of Christ shine in your heart, He will light up your life.

**"In him was life, and the life was the light of men."
John 1:4**

I AM…shining brightly for you to see more clearly. I am the light of the world. Only I can bring light to the darkness and give you the truth when you draw closer to My light. Step out of the dark into the marvelous light of My love.

Are you in the dark?

Follow Me; I will light the way for you so you can see My illuminated path that is right in front of you. The light glistens and shines as rays of My love soak into your soul. Trust Me to light up your life!

Where do you need light in your life right now?

Come out of the darkness and into God's marvelous light where God will show you the way.

Faith rises when fear disappears.

"For I, the LORD your God, hold your right hand; it is I who say to you, 'Fear not, I am the one who helps you.'"
Isaiah 41:13

I AM…the one who will help you. All you need, I will provide. Trust Me to take away all your fear and increase your faith. I have chosen you and set you apart to be *fearless*. I will hold your right hand as you surrender and let Me lead you. There is no need to fear what might happen, but there is more room to ask for My help.

Where do you need help?

Ask, and I will carry you and shelter you in My arms. I will not let go of you, dear one. Rest in My loving arms and find comfort for your weary soul.

Fear or faith?

Which one is more prevalent in your life right now?

Why?

I
AM
THE
MESSIAH

Look to Jesus as you run your race and His joy will be with you all the way home.

"Let us run with endurance the race that is set before us, looking to Jesus, the founder and perfecter of our faith, who for the joy that was set before him endured the cross…"
Hebrews 12:1-2

I AM…hovering in protection over you but you do not see Me. Your eyes are on the problem and not Me. I have bubble-wrapped you in My prayers. I will not let you go but will strengthen you for what is to come.

Do you need strength?

I will strengthen you as you run with Me. I will give you endurance to run swiftly. Do not try to figure it all out by yourself. Trust Me because I have the plan in the palm of My hand, perfectly made just for you!

Do you see God's hand in your plan?

If not, ask Him to show you.

When you are with Christ, you become citizens of the greatest Kingdom.

"But our citizenship is in heaven, and from it we await a Savior, the Lord Jesus Christ."
Philippians 3:20

I AM…granting you citizenship in My Kingdom as you come to Me with arms wide open ready to find your salvation in Me. With My freedom, you are free.

Will you make the choice to follow Me to new life and freedom?

You will never regret making the choice to be Mine. You are not alone. I am near you. You are a citizen of My great Kingdom. Make the choice to love Me. Let Me save you. We will walk together and live in love and peace, forever.

Are you lonely?

God wants to be your friend so you will never walk alone.

Let go and let God do more in you.

"I know your works. Behold, I have set before you an open door, which no one is able to shut."
Revelation 3:8

I AM...able to do more in you. Let Me show you what I can do. I will open doors for you that have been shut. I will take control of impossible situations and make a way where there is not one. I will help you in your struggles and give you victories in your battles.

Do you know that I have already won the victory for you?

All you must do is let go and let Me work in you. Give everything over to Me, so I can do far more abundantly than all you could ask or think.

What door do you need God to open for you?

Write a prayer asking God to show you the open door.

Listen to the gentle whisper and you will know which way to go.

"For as the heavens are higher than the earth, so are my ways higher than your ways and my thoughts than your thoughts."
Isaiah 55:9

I AM...speaking truth to you. Open your heart and listen. I have so much to tell you. My thoughts are higher and deeper than your own. You are searching far and wide for things that only I can tell you.

Do you hear Me?

Listen with love, and the darkness will not overcome you. I have overcome the world. Open the window of your soul and let My light in. Look up and see the glorious things only I can show you. The light will enter in as you open the window to your heart.

What is God whispering to you?

If you hear His voice, thank Him. If you do not, be still and listen.

Where there is pain, there is hope with Jesus.

"I appeal to you therefore, brothers, by the mercies of God, to present your bodies as a living sacrifice, holy and acceptable to God, which is your spiritual worship."
Romans 12:1

I AM…living in you. Present your body as a living sacrifice to Me by worshipping me joyfully no matter what your circumstances may be. I know what you are going through. I have been broken, just like you. I have been persecuted, just like you. I have wept, just like you. I feel your pain and know your struggles.

But do you know the good news?

I have suffered so you can be set free from sin! I have sacrificed all so you can have life. Surrender all to Me. I am living in you so that you can live eternally!

Are you living in the moment or stressing about the future?

Ask God to give you peace in the present.

His love is our gift, wrapped and sealed with a timeless bow.

"Who shall separate us from the love of Christ?"
Romans 8:35

I AM...close to your heart. Make room for Me and know that nothing can separate you from My love. I see that others have hurt you and even tried to make you feel worthless. But I say you are worthy and loved. I will not leave or abandon you like others have. I will be your anchor.

Do you know how much I love you?

Close your eyes and breathe. You are Mine. Rest in the promise of My everlasting love and let Me hold you. You are precious to Me.

Are you making room for God in your life?

If not, how can you do that beginning today?

If so, do you feel his joy today?

Let His roots grow deeper in you so that your faith will bloom in the rich soil of His love.

"Therefore, as you have received Christ Jesus the Lord, so walk in him, rooted and built up in him and established in the faith, just as you were taught, abounding in thanksgiving."
Colossians 2:6-7

I AM…growing in you as your faith is planted in Me. Keep Me first and walk where I will lead you. I have wonderful plans for you that you will soon see. You are one decision away from total peace and joy.

Will you decide to follow Me?

Give Me all and you will be on track for abundant blessings. Do not be distracted but keep singing the victory song I put on your heart. Worship Me, and I will carry you home!

Is God first in your life?

He wants all of you, not just some. Make a commitment to give Him more.

When the Lord is your shepherd, you will be safe and sheltered.

"The LORD is my shepherd; I shall not want."
Psalm 23:1

I AM…your Good Shepherd. Hear My voice and find shelter in Me. I will lead you where it is safe and watch over you as I lead you to green pastures and still waters. There is no place you can go that I will not be present. You cannot hide from Me. I will find you even when you are lost.

Are you crying out to Me?

I can heal You. I hear your cries for help. I will bring you out of the wilderness and into My presence. Carefully listen to My voice, for I am calling you Mine, once and for all.

Did you know that God hears your cries for help?

Keep praying to the God who heals broken hearts and lost souls.

Exalt God with your praises and magnify His name with your prayers.

**"Oh, magnify the LORD with me, let us exalt his name together!"
Psalm 34:3**

I AM…so very close to you. Everywhere you look for Me, you will find Me near to you. I am present all around you. Look for Me and seek Me wherever you go. Search for Me in the stillness and in the chaos.

Do you see Me?

I will never leave you because I love you. Lift your praises and your prayers to Me. I am ready to give you so much more than you will ever need. Speak to Me. I am listening.

What is on your heart to pray about today?

Write your prayers and praise God for His answers.

Let every step you take be in step with the Spirit.

**"If we live by the Spirit, let us also keep in step with the Spirit."
Galatians 5:25**

I AM...walking with you to victory. Keep in step with Me. I have so much to show you, dear child. You are so beautiful with My Spirit living in you. I know the cares of the world are trying to pull you away from Me, but nothing can separate us when My Spirit is in you.

Are you drawing nearer to Me or giving up because life is hard?

Do not give up. Keep your head up and your heart close to Mine. I love to see you living in the power of the Spirit. Life in the Spirit is the only way to live!

Are you living in the power of the Holy Spirit?

Close your eyes and let the Spirit bring you peace right now.

Stand on the solid rock and you will stand firm in freedom.

"For freedom Christ has set us free; stand firm therefore, and do not submit again to a yoke of slavery."
Galatians 5:1

I AM...the key to your complete freedom. All you have to say is, "Yes, I want to be free," and then yoke yourself to Me. I need your complete trust. Drop the yoke that is holding you captive and take hold of Me.

Will you take My hand and let Me hold you?

I am here for you. I love you. Receive My love and let it cover the parts of you that need more of Me. I will fill you to the fullest and give you freedom.

Why are you not letting go of all that is holding you captive?

List these things and commit to let them go today.

When you let go, God will lift you up.

"Because he holds fast to me in love, I will deliver him; I will protect him, because he knows my name."
Psalm 91:14

I AM...the lifter of your head. I am waiting for you to let go and let Me deliver you. You have been letting so many things weigh and press you down. Give Me those weights and I will make your load lighter, and your cares go away.

What concerns are you still holding onto?

Remember, you are not the only one in this battle. I will fight for you and take every worry and concern if you release *all* to Me. I love you, dear one. We are in this together.

Write a prayer of surrender to the Lord.

Pray this prayer and feel God's presence over you today.

Open your heart and your ears to the sound of God's whisper as you pray.

"But truly God has listened; he has attended to the voice of my prayer." Psalm 66:19

I AM…listening to you. Make time for Me through prayer. I can hear your requests and I will answer you. I will speak, if you will listen to My voice. Stop listening to all the other voices pulling you away from Me. You have been ignoring My gentle whisper and have been distracted by everyone else.

Will you let Me speak life into you?

I have your best interest at heart because I love you. Believe this and keep talking to Me. I want to be your friend. I hear you as you pray. Don't stop believing. I have not given up on you!

Do you feel like God has given up on you?

Know that He hears you and will never give up on you. Pray right now that you would listen to receive His love.

Hearts will be softened when Christ is chosen.

**"And I will give you a new heart, and a new spirit I will put within you. And I will remove the heart of stone from your flesh and give you a heart of flesh."
Ezekiel 36:26**

I AM…wanting to put a new heart of flesh within you. The old heart of stone will be removed, and the new heart of flesh will grow inside you as you make the call to have it all. Make Me the Lord of your life. I am the only one who can truly soften your heart.

Will you choose Me?

The other things you have made your priority have interfered with the treasures I want to give you. I have a new spirit to put in you, so let Me in your heart.

God wants you to make Him the Lord of your life.

Have you made the decision to follow Him so He can soften your heart today?

Commit your way to *the* Way.

"Well done, good servant! Because you have been faithful in a very little, you shall have authority over ten cities."
Luke 19:17

I AM...eager to see your face, My child. Look to Me so I can shine My light on you. I see all the ways you have been working to please Me. I know you are trying to follow the path I have put before you.

What path will you follow?

It is good to see you working for My glory and honor. I am so proud of you, dear child. You have made sacrifices to see My face. You have been faithful in little, so I want to grant you more opportunities to grow My kingdom. Keep looking at Me, for I love you.

Do you wonder if God will say to you, "well done, good servant?"

List some ways you are working for His kingdom today and believe He is well pleased with you.

I
AM
HE

When you seek the Lord, you will find Him.

"In peace I will both lie down and sleep; for you alone, O Lord, make me dwell in safety."
Psalm 4:8

I AM...proud of you, dear child, because you never stop seeking Me. I am nearer to you than when you first believed. I draw closer when you call upon Me. I will carry you through the flood and the fire. Just close your eyes and say My name. Rest in My love for you.

Will you look to Me for your peace?

Dear child, I will bring peace to your soul and your problems will fade. Focus on Me and not the storm. I am greater than anything you will ever face! Now, lie down with Me in your heart and mind and you will feel safe and secure.

Close your eyes and speak the name above all names, Jesus Christ.

Now let His peace wash over you today.

When you put on love, God wraps you up with His bow.

"And above all these put on love, which binds everything together in perfect harmony."
Colossians 3:14

I AM…covering you with My love. Each time you think of Me, breathe in My love for you. Know how much I love you, dear child. I want you to feel special and share in the peace that exists with Me. I know there are problems that have weighed heavily on your heart.

Will you let Me help you?

I can help fix all of those if you let Me. Love will bind everything together in perfect harmony. Let My love in and open Your heart to more of Me.

Have you thought about how much God loves you?

Turn on some praise music today and feel the power of His love as you worship your Father.

Prayer changes things, but it mostly changes you as you grow closer to God.

**"Continue steadfastly in prayer, being watchful in it with thanksgiving."
Colossians 4:2**

I AM…listening to you as you pray. I see your faithfulness and will speak to you. Come closer to Me, dear child. I have glorious things to tell you that you have not heard yet. I believe you are ready to receive all that I have for you, faithful one.

What do you need from Me?

Those things you have been praying for have touched Me. I am open to give at the right time. Be watchful, be thankful, and praise Me for what is coming!

What has been a prayer that you continue praying day by day?

Write it here, and pray, believing God will answer. Praise Him for He is a good Father!

There is no darkness when you walk with Jesus.

**"Again Jesus spoke to them saying, "I am the light of the world. Whoever follows me will not walk in darkness, but will have the light of life."
John 8:12**

I AM…your light. Come to Me and let Me light up your life. I have brightened the dark places with the light of My everlasting and brilliant love. You can step out of the dark if you choose to follow Me.

Are you walking in the dark or into the light?

Just walk out into My light and feel the warmth all over you. There is no darkness at all with Me. Only I can help you see. Look, for I am right there with you, showing you the way out. I am leading you. Follow Me.

Where do you need God's light to shine so He can light up your life?

Ask God to show you the lighted path as you pray today.

Live with fresh faith because God is always faithful.

**"He who calls you is faithful; he will surely do it."
1 Thessalonians 5:24**

I AM…faithful to you, dear child. I can do the impossible for you. Pray and listen to My truth, then put your feet to your faith and stand firm with Me. You have been backsliding for some time now. It is time to come back to the foundation you know and let go of the things that are taking you away from Me.

Do you believe all things are possible with Me?

I need your whole heart so I can make it possible. Remember, I am always faithful. Now stay faithful to Me so I can do more in you.

Pause and pray.

What is God speaking to you today?

God already knows when you are in need of prayer.

**"The LORD is near to the brokenhearted and saves the crushed in spirit."
Psalm 34:18**

I AM...near to you. I hear Your prayers and I see your broken heart. I will save your crushed spirit if you draw nearer to Me. I will not let go of you. I have seen all your tears and I have wept with you. I know the pain you feel and the trials you are facing. My heart breaks for you. But I can heal you.

Will you let Me heal you?

The only answer for your brokenness is to draw even closer to Me. I will hold you and comfort you through it *all,* dear one. Hold My hand and let Me rescue you. When you believe, I will never let you go.

What is breaking your heart right now?

Pray to release it to God and picture Him holding you.

When you put your feet to faith your steps will be blessed.

"I press on toward the goal for the prize of the upward call of God in Christ Jesus." Philippians 3:14

I AM...your cherished prize. Make room for Me to work in you, dear child. When you look to Me, I will give you the strength you need to press on.

Are you too concerned with your circumstances that you have forgotten to focus on Me?

I know life can be hard, that is why I need you to trust Me wholeheartedly. I will empower you in the most beautiful ways. I will lift you up as you let go. Say yes and be blessed!

What struggle are you facing today?

Write it down here and give it to God.

Lift your head up because only God can shield you from the storm.

**"But you, O LORD, are a shield about me, my glory, and the lifter of my head."
Psalm 3:3**

I AM…the lifter of your head. Look up, child. Let Me help you. I see you and will put My shield around you so that nothing can harm you. That surmounting problem that has you distressed is nothing for Me. Think about the ways I have helped you in the past.

Do you remember what I have done for you?

Now, release your stress, look up to Me, and believe that I will do what I have promised you. Have faith in Me and My promises. I can help you through it, if you will let Me do it!

What problem seems too hard for you right now?

Will you let God work it out for you?

If so, write a prayer releasing it to God.

Your desires come to life when God is the love of your life.

**"Commit your way to the LORD: trust in him, and he will act."
Psalm 37:5**

I AM…watching you love with an open heart, just as I have loved you. As you delight in spending more time with Me each day, My desires will be implanted in you. What I want for you will come to life, as you grow to know Me. I want to be close to you so I can show you the blessings I have in store for you.

Will you stay closer to Me?

I hear you praying. I see you serving. I know you are reading My Word. I will put My Spirit within you. Watch Me change you as you put Me first!

How have you spent time with God today?

What are the desires of your heart?

Pray to know the way.

"The prayer of a righteous person has great power as it is working."
James 5:16

I AM…listening as you pray. I do hear you. I know it seems like My answers may be slow to you, but take heart, I know the perfect timing for what must happen. I have your best interest at heart. You are Mine and I love you. I will take care of every concern when you give Me time to answer you.

What prayers are you waiting for Me to answer?

My glory shines brightest when you let Me hold you. Don't let go. Keep the prayers coming. Learn to love the wait, because I am in every moment.

What are you waiting for?

Have you continued praying?

Lift up your faithful prayers right now.

When God is your life, He is your best friend.

**"I will praise you with an upright heart,
when I learn your righteous rules."
Psalm 119:7**

I AM…leading you to the place where I am. When you praise Me with an upright heart, I am well pleased. All you have to do is call Me, and I will be there. In fact, I am already right where you need Me. I am just waiting on you to let Me in.

Do you need a little nudge to open up your heart?

I will nurture your soul and open your heart. Come closer, dear child, I am waiting patiently for you to receive Me with open arms and a willing heart.

Praise the Lord for He is so good.

Tell Him how much you love Him and write what you hear Him tell you.

Seek the Lord with your whole heart and you will find Him.

"**God is faithful, and he will not let you be tempted beyond your ability, but with the temptation he will also provide the way of escape, that you may be able to endure it.**"
1 Corinthians 10:13

I AM…your Helper. Make room for Me and listen to my commandments. I will direct you to the truth and give you courage to keep on the straight path. I know you have temptations surrounding you and it is hard to say no. But when you say yes to Me, I will provide a way out for you.

Where are you being tempted right now?

Listen to the still, small voice inside guiding you to truth, and obey what your heart knows to be true. Turn away from the other voices and let Me help you.

Is there something that keeps tempting you that you know is not from God?

Write it down and let it go today. Do you feel free?

Joy flows continuously when God is present in your life.

"Count it all joy, my brothers, when you meet trials of various kinds, for you know that the testing of your faith produces steadfastness."
James 1:2-3

I AM…your joy even in the trials of life. Take heart, I have overcome the world for you. I want to save you and make you whole again. There is nothing too hard for Me.

What is troubling you?

Look to Me and flee from the problem. When you come closer to My love, My joy will flow through you no matter what circumstances come your way. That trial will strengthen your faith. So, start counting joy, and your life will change, indeed!

Are you or someone you know going through a trial right now?

Write it here and pray that God will strengthen your faith and increase your joy.

Come closer to the one who is close to you.

**"Then you will call upon me and come and pray to me, and I will hear you."
Jeremiah 29:12**

I AM... close to you. Take My hand and let Me renew you. There is hope and joy where I am. Do not lose heart but turn your heart towards Me again. I know you are hurting and feel isolated, but I promise to help you get through this storm.

What storm has come your way?

Come closer, listen to My voice, turn to Me, and I will help you navigate your way, so you are not walking alone. Lift your prayers to Me, take My hand, and hold Me tighter. Believe that if I have brought you to it, I will bring you through it.

Have you isolated yourself from others and from God? How will you come closer to Him?

Take a moment and reflect on how much God does love you. Now pray and praise Him for loving you so much that He gave His Son so that you can have forgiveness for your sins.

When your heart is close to the Lord, your mouth will praise Him.

"Let the words of my mouth and the meditation of my heart be acceptable in your sight, O LORD, my rock and my redeemer."
Psalm 19:14

I AM...your firm foundation. Trust Me to be your rock. Stand strong with Me so I can give you the words to speak. I know you are afraid of what you might say, but shift your focus to Me, and I will guide your thoughts and your heart to the truth.

Is your focus on Me?

Turn towards Me and stand on the promises that I have given you. Let your actions speak louder than your words. I will be your very present help wherever you go, and I will help you speak what is pleasing to Me.

What promise of God are you standing on today?

Speak it over yourself and speak it to someone else God puts on your heart.

Love is the key that opens the heart.

**"Love never ends. As for prophecies, they will pass away; as for tongues, they will cease, as for knowledge it will pass away."
1 Corinthians 13:8**

I AM...full of love for you. Do not fret over the issues before you, dear one. My love will comfort you. My love will shelter you. Take heart and follow me to freedom and love. I am only a prayer away. Listen to the heartbeat of My love for you.

Are you listening?

Now, fully surrender by giving Me your heart and let Me love you unconditionally. Hear the gentle whispers of My love that never ends; it lasts forever without fail. I love you, my beloved. Receive My love with a joyful heart.

Have you surrendered all to your loving God?

Pray a prayer of surrender and thank God for loving you.

Those who let the Lord shepherd them will never be lost.

**"My sheep hear my voice, and I know them, and they follow me."
John 10:27**

I AM...watching over you, my dear child. Stay in My sheepfold and let Me protect you. I have all that you need. I will provide for you and hide you in My shelter. Listen to My voice and follow Me.

Do you need a hiding place?

Come to Me and rest your weary body. I will protect you and keep you secure. Those other distractions will disappear when you come closer to Me. Stay with Me. Feel My protective love cover you from any danger and hear My voice show you the way to go. With Me, you will never be lost again. For I am your Good Shepherd.

Is there a distraction that has taken you away from God's presence?

Write it here and pray to let it go so God can hold you close.

We can make our plans, but the Lord makes our way.

"Many are the plans in the mind of a man, but it is the purpose of the LORD that will stand."
Proverbs 19:21

I AM...making a way for you. Let Me show you the plans I have for you with My purpose in mind. I can do what seems impossible if you let Me work. You have been running and gunning with your plans for so long. If you let Me, I can rewrite the plans for your good and My glory.

Will you give Me total control instead of focusing only on yourself?

When I am your focus, things will work out. Keep your eyes on Me, and I will give you the strength to go through it. Release control to Me and see what happens.

Are there plans that you have made without seeking God?

If so, write them here and seek God for His plan and purpose. Then pray for His will to be done in you.

When God is in your heart, He will be in your house.

**"But as for me and my house, we will serve the LORD."
Joshua 24:15**

I AM...close to your heart and in your house when I am Lord of your life. I will come and live with you when you let Me in. Surrender all, and I will be present with you and in you.

Have you made the choice to let me dwell with you?

Make room for Me by opening the door to your heart. I am always there for you, dear child. When you dwell with Me, I see you. When you call Me, I hear you. When you seek Me, I know you. When you ask for forgiveness, I forgive you. Make Me the Lord of your life and see how much I love you.

Where are you serving the Lord?

Are you serving Him in your house?

The Lord delights to rescue and support you.

"But the LORD was my support. He brought me out into a broad place; he rescued me, because he delighted in me." 2 Samuel 22:19-20

I AM...your refuge and strength. Do not turn away from Me. Keep Me close to you and hold Me tight so I can help you. I see how much you are hurting. There are some who have betrayed you, even those who are closest to you. I am sorry you are going through this struggle.

Will you let it go?

I will touch you with My healing power of love. I will never fail you, dear child. Hold on to Me so I can rescue and comfort you and give you hope once again.

Is there someone who has hurt you recently?

Write their name down, pray for them, and forgive them.

The more you pray, the sweeter your life becomes.

"Let my prayer be counted as incense before you, and the lifting up of my hands as the evening sacrifice!"
Psalm 141:2

I AM...listening to your prayers. I have heard your heart as you pray. I know the deep needs of your soul. I will give you your heart's desire when your heart is right before Me. As you share your love with me through prayer, I will come to you. I will meet you where you are and comfort you with My peace and provision.

Will you keep praying?

My will is for you to love Me and trust Me in all circumstances. Your prayers fill the atmosphere with the sweetest aroma. I will meet you in the place where you pray.

How often do you pray?

Take more time to pray each day. God will bless your life richly as you pray and thank Him for His answers.

Walk with the Son and you will shine.

"For the LORD God is a sun and a shield; the LORD bestows favor and honor. No good thing does he withhold from those who walk uprightly."
Psalm 84:11

I AM...shining brilliantly in your heart as you make Me Lord of your life. I will shield you and honor you with My protective love. Nothing can harm you when your armor is on. I am surrounding you and will fight for you.

Will you let Me shield you?

I will lead you to victory, as My child, bestowed with strength and dignity from above. I have conquered death for you on the cross. Nothing is impossible for Me. Believe I will do it and receive all I have for you. My glory shines brightly in those who walk uprightly.

What battle are you fighting right now?

Have you let God fight for you?

When you are with God, He will not pass you by.

**"Man is like a breath; his days are like a passing shadow."
Psalm 144:4**

I AM…the very breath you breathe. I have put My Spirit inside you to give you peace and life everlasting. You can rest in My presence knowing that I can infuse you with power for the days ahead. Your days are passing by rapidly, so make the most of every moment I give you. Make time for those who need you.

Will you follow Me instead of your shadow?

Stop thinking of yourself first and think of Me. When you love Me, you can love everyone. It is possible to love and serve others when My love is first in your life.

Who needs the love of Jesus today?

Pray for them and go serve them with the love that flows from Jesus.

When you dwell with the Lord, your home will be His heart.

"Because you have made the LORD your dwelling place, the Most High, who is my refuge, no evil shall be allowed to befall you, no plague come near your tent." Psalm 91:9-10

I AM…your home. You do not have to worry about evil when the Son lives in your heart. I will guard you from any harm when you are connected to Me. I only want the best for you, for My will to be done in your life. I have overcome the world for you.

Do you realize that nothing can come between you and Me when I am Lord of your life?

I will comfort you in the hardest of times. My goodness and mercy always prevail. Turn toward Me and make me your dwelling place.

What difficult situation is before you?

Commit your heart to dwell with God instead of dwelling on the problems.

When you abide in Jesus, He speaks to your heart.

"I am the vine; you are the branches. Whoever abides in me and I in him, he it is that bears much fruit, for apart from me you can do nothing."
John 15:5

I AM…close to you because you are abiding in Me. You are fruitful as you continue seeking Me. I am listening to your heart and will attend to the voice of your prayer. Let go of those distractions that are pulling you away from Me.

Will you come closer to Me?

Abide and listen to me so you can find hope in what I say. Believe that you are worthy and so loved. I have your best interest at heart, and I am your best Yes. Keep abiding and you will find joy everlasting!

Are you abiding daily in Jesus?

What or who is keeping you from a closer relationship with Him?

I
AM
LIVING
WATER

It is better to give than to receive.

**"Each one must give as he has decided in his heart, not reluctantly or under compulsion for God loves a cheerful giver."
2 Corinthians 9:7**

I AM…pleased with you as I see you give. You are spreading joy by sharing My love. The recipients of your gifts will know Me when you love them. Keep doing all that you are doing for Me with gladness and cheerfulness. I have seen your giving hands and feet working for My Kingdom.

Do you find My joy when you give?

My joy will come to you in so many ways as you give. You will be amazed at what I will do in the hearts of My people. Look up, and do not give up doing good for a harvest of blessings is coming for you!

Who can you bless with your gifts?

Pray that God will show you those who need you and then do what He has called you to do.

Love God first and let Him love you so you can love others well.

**"Beloved, let us love one another, for love is from God, and whoever loves has been born of God and knows God."
1 John 4:7**

I AM…full of the utmost love for you, my child. I see you and I know you. Do you see and know Me? Will you love Me as I love you? I am here for you and will help you through everything. Trust Me to guide you. Give Me your hand so I can hold you.

Will you let go and be loved?

With My steady love, you will be secure and be able to love others well. This world needs more love. I promise to be with you always. All you must do is say Yes to My love and I will come after you.

Do you know God's redeeming love?

Close your eyes and feel the warmth of His love for you.

The more you pray and praise, the less you panic about your problems.

**"Rejoice always, pray without ceasing, give thanks in all circumstances, for this is the will of God in Christ Jesus for you."
1 Thessalonians 5:16-18**

I AM…eagerly awaiting your prayers and praises. Keep those prayers coming and do not stop giving thanks for the answers I give you. I will answer when you pray. My answers come in My timing and My will for you. I see the big picture and know what is to come.

Will you give it all to Me?

Trust Me to help you and do not give up hope. Rejoice before the answer comes and pray with faith that it will happen. And do not stop asking, seeking, and knocking so I can open the door to your good and My glory!

What prayer is awaiting answers for you right now?

Have you praised God for the answer before it comes? Praise God from who all blessings flow!

Live a life of holiness with God and you will be blessed with His shield of favor.

"For you bless the righteous; O LORD; you cover him with favor as with a shield." Psalm 5:12

I AM...waiting for you to live the life I have for you. I am nearer to you than when you first believed. I brought you to a place of freedom and hope. Now, live in righteousness with Me by obeying My commands and trusting Me in all circumstances. I will provide a way out when you are tempted and lack self-control. I will show you the way when you seek Me and listen to My voice.

Are you listening to my voice or to others?

I will direct your mind and guard your heart. My favor will cover you as a shield when you live connected to Me. Come closer, dear child.

Do you feel near to God right now?

Tell Him you love Him and seek repentance for things that you need to change that are keeping you farther away from Him.

Stand on the promises of God and you will be able to stand firm.

**"I am the way, and the truth, and the life."
John 14:6**

I AM…your promise keeper. Stand on My promises. When you trust in Me, there is so much I can do for, and with, you. I will set you free again.

Remember when you first confessed your sins and made the choice to believe that I sacrificed My Son for you?

Come back to Me and let Me love you. I have forgiven you, dear child. There is nothing you have done that would take away My love. I will break those chains you have attached to yourself. My way is the way to a life of freedom and peace. Stand with Me and you will never stand alone!

What sin are you still chained to?

Let Christ break it for you by confessing it to Him. Now let it go and let Him love you again.

God fills us with love through His gifting of the Holy Spirit to all who believe and receive.

"God's love has been poured into our hearts through the Holy Spirit who has been given to us."
Romans 5:5

I AM…gifting you with My Spirit, dear one. You received because you have believed. I love to give gifts to My children. Now, as you listen to My still, small voice, you will know which direction to take and which path to pursue. I will not lead you astray but will tell you what to do as you pray.

Are you asking Me and listening for My answers?

Keep asking, and you shall receive. I sealed you with the Holy Spirit when you asked Jesus Christ inside your heart. Listen to the Truth and do what has been asked of you!

Do you hear the still, small voice of the Holy Spirit encouraging you?

Pray to hear Him and obey His promptings as you listen with your heart.

Waiting on God gives you time to experience how wonderful He really is.

"The LORD is good to those who wait for him, to the soul who seeks him."
Lamentations 3:25

I AM…a calming presence for your soul. Wait upon Me so I can direct your path. Live in the moment with Me. Let Me encourage you with My promises. Have faith in Me. I know you are a planner and want to see every detail. But with Me, you can rest with confidence knowing that I will work things out in ways you cannot even imagine.

Do you believe I have something better for you?

I love you and want the very best for you, my beloved. Open your heart and seek Me so I can do good for you. My love will enrich your beautiful soul.

What are you waiting for right now?

Are you stressing about it or focusing on the promises of God?

Read the promise in the scripture today and believe God is so good to you.

When you seek God and look to Him for all you need, He will revive you.

"I lift my eyes to the hills. From where does my help come? My help comes from the LORD, who made heaven and earth." Psalm 121:1-2

I AM...your constant help. I do what seems impossible for you. Let go and let Me revive you. Tell Me what is on your heart and trust Me to tend to you. I see you. I hear you. I love you. I know what has been heavy on your heart. I am your way to freedom.

Have you looked to Me for all you need?

Lay it all down and quit worrying about all those things. I have already worked them out and am just waiting for you to let go. Give it all to Me. Nothing you are facing is impossible for Me. If you believe, look up, child!

Have you looked to God to help you with what you are facing today?

Write down your worries and turn them into a prayer list.

Mountain-moving faith begins and ends with God.

"For truly I say to you, if you have faith like a grain of mustard seed, you will say to this mountain, 'Move from here to there, and it will move, and nothing will be impossible for you.'"
Matthew 17:20

I AM…waiting for you to put your full faith in Me. I want to be your Good Shepherd, to lead you beside still waters so you can drink of My living water and be refreshed forever. I am right here.

Have you asked Me to live in your heart?

My Son will bring His light of salvation and give you the Holy Spirit to live inside of you. The only way to have all this is through Me, your loving Father. Seek Me and live and I will give you faith to move mountains.

Do you want faith that can move mountains?

When you seek more of God, He will increase your faith and revive your heart. End this devotional by writing a love letter to your Heavenly Father and pray that you will keep seeking God for everything.

Looking for More?

A Year of Daily Devotionals for One-on-One Time with God

Available on Amazon
https://www.amazon.com/dp/B08LTRBDN5

God-Size Your Prayers to Find Your Destiny

Prayers FROM THE HEART

Available on Amazon
https://www.amazon.com/dp/B07TW7YMHV

Also By Jill Lowry

A Year of Daily Devotionals to
Ignite Your Heart for Jesus

Available on Amazon
https://www.amazon.com/dp/B07HKK2MN9

Promises of HOPE

Available on Amazon
https://www.amazon.com/dp/B09NBCTPSP

Available on Amazon
https://www.amazon.com/dp/B079VTNMY9

Available Here:
https://www.amazon.com/dp/B093XY7HPZ

Prayer Journals also Available on Amazon

https://www.amazon.com/dp/1693027763

https://www.amazon.com/dp/0578633906

ABOUT THE AUTHOR

Jill Lowry is an ardent follower of Jesus who has a desire and passion to communicate His truth as inspired by the Holy Spirit. Her writings combine the accuracy of a scholar with the practicality of a wife and mother. Jill grew up in San Antonio, Texas. She graduated from the University of Texas with a Bachelor of Business Administration in Marketing and holds a law degree from St. Mary's University School of Law.

Jill is the founder and president of a student mentoring and food program, Mt Vernon Cares, created for at-risk students at the local high school. She is the host of a faith-based weekly radio talk show and podcast, "Real Life Real People Radio." She also hosts a new podcast of three minute devotionals, called "Seek God," and co-hosts another podcast where two friends share coffee and Jesus conversations to inspire others on their journey of faith called "Journey with Jesus." Listen to these on Apple, Google, Spotify, Podbean and Soundcloud.

Jill takes every opportunity to pray with friends and neighbors in need and considers intercessory prayer a vital part of her ministry. She is part of a weekly community prayer group which meets to pray for revival in her community and beyond.

Her desire and prayer is that you will be encouraged to find your joy in Jesus through the application of scripture and truth from the Holy Spirit found in her books, journals, devotionals, and prayers, as well as her radio show and podcasts.

Visit her website for more information on these ministries and subscribe to receive inspirational daily prayers.

http://www.jilllowryministries.com

If you enjoy podcasts, you can listen to my podcast, **SEEK GOD,** a podcast of 3 minute devotionals on Apple, Spotify, Goggle and Podbean podcasts.

https://podcasts.apple.com/us/podcast/id1649067547

www.ingramcontent.com/pod-product-compliance
Lightning Source LLC
LaVergne TN
LVHW051548070426
835507LV00021B/2469